Battle OF THE SeXes ™

Warning: Small parts may be a choking hazard. Not for children under 3 years.

ACKNOWLEDGEMENTS

A big thanks to all those who worked so hard (and so fast!) on this project
Writing/research team: Erin Conley, Cherie A. Martorana, Lani Stackel, Maria Llull,
Katie Ranftle, and Bob Moog
Editing team: Erin Conley, Heather Russell-Revesz, Rick Campbell, and Bob Moog
Proofing/fact-checking team: Heather Russell-Revesz, Rick Campbell,
Suzanne Cracraft, and Lani Stackel
Design/production team: Jeff Batzli, Richela Morgan, and Michael Friedman
Sales and promotions team: Jules Herbert, Bruce Lubin, Mary Carlomagno,
and Michael Friedman
We couldn't have done it without you!

Design: Lindgren/Fuller Design

ISBN 1-57528-905-9

03 04 MC 9 8 7 6 5 4 3

CONTENTS

ABOUT THE AUTHOR

Always ahead of the game, Bob Moog's newest undertaking is truly novel. As a game inventor, his credits include such favorites as Twenty Questions® and 30 Second Mysteries®. As the CEO of University Games, he has propelled the company he founded with his college pal into an international operation that now boasts five divisions and over 350 products. Whether hosting his radio show "Games People Play," advising MBA candidates, or inventing games, Bob sees work as serious fun. He now brings his flair for fun and learning to the bookshelf with the Spinner Book line.

RULES OF PLAY

For 2 or more players.

OBJECT

To be the first team to earn 15 points—and find out how much you really know about the opposite sex!

PLAYING THE GAME

- First things first: grab a pen and paper to keep track of your points.
- Divide players into two teams: men vs. women.
- The men spin first to determine which sex will get to answer a set of questions. A set consists of three questions. (In other words, all the questions on the page!)

  - If the spinner lands on the **men only** zone, a player from the women's team reads the men the first set of questions from the men's question section.
  - If the spinner lands on the **women only** zone, a player from the men's team reads the women the first set of questions from the women's question section.
  - If the spinner lands on the **both sexes** zone, a player from the women's team reads the men a set of questions from the men's question section.

Then a player from the men's team reads the women a set of questions from the women's question section.

- *Teams earn one point for each question answered correctly.* (For example, if the men answer 2 questions right, they get 2 points. The maximum a team may earn in a given round is 3 points. Got it? Good!)

- Play now continues and the women take a spin.

WINNING THE GAME

The first team to earn 15 points wins the Battle of the Sexes—and the right to gloat until the next game!

Men's
Questions

Q: What is the name of the popular wool woven from the undercoat of the Himalayan mountain goat?

A: Pashmina

Q: In the Grimm's fairy tale, who is Snow White's sister?

A: Rose Red

Q: What Olympian made the "wedge" a sassy and stylish haircut in the 1970s?

A: Dorothy Hamill

 Q: What type of flower is an American Beauty?

A: Rose

 Q: Name three of the four Cs used to determine a diamond's quality.

A: Cut, clarity, carat, and color

 Q: Which pasta doesn't have a filling: tortellini, ravioli, or rigatoni?

A: Rigatoni

 Q: If you are buying a dress that is size 6P, what does the "P" stand for?

A: Petite

 Q: What is the name of the reddish orange-colored seasoning, made from sweet red peppers, used to top deviled eggs?

A: Paprika

 Q: Who is Raggedy Ann's brother?

A: Raggedy Andy

Q: What television network features programs like *Intimate Portrait* and *Women Docs*?

A: Lifetime

Q: What type of pantyhose provides firm elastic support around the stomach?

A: Control Top

Q: Which has the most calories: a blueberry muffin from Starbucks, a small fries from McDonald's, or a Mrs. Fields milk chocolate-chip cookie?

A: A blueberry muffin from Starbucks (weighing in with 380 calories!)

 Q: Iyengar, Bikram, and Ashtanga are all types of what?

A: Yoga

 Q: What comedienne hosts E! Entertainment Television's live Oscars® pre-show with her daughter?

A: Joan Rivers

 Q: Downy, Snuggle, and Bounce are all brand names for what type of household product?

A: Fabric softener

Q: When shopping for linens, what should one always consider in order to ensure the highest quality?

A: The thread count

Q: What color is vermilion: yellowish green, reddish orange, or violet?

A: Reddish orange

Q: What four schoolgirls learned "the facts of life" in a popular 1980s sitcom of the same name?

A: Blair, Tootie, Natalie, and Jo

Q: What female jazz singer had her first major hit with "A-Tisket, A-Tasket" in 1938?

A: Ella Fitzgerald

Q: How long should you keep mascara: three months, six months, or a year?

A: Three months

Q: Name two of the four March sisters in *Little Women*.

A: Meg, Jo, Beth, and Amy

Q: What U.S. gymnast made headlines—and scored Olympic gold—when she vaulted with an injured ankle at the 1996 Summer Games?

A: Kerri Strug

Q: When setting a place at a table, what side does the wine glass go on?

A: The right

Q: In the 1995 romantic comedy *Clueless*, Alicia Silverstone played a character named after what famous singer?

A: Cher

 Q: What plant's thick, aromatic root flavors Chinese dishes, soda pop, and "snaps"?

A: Ginger

 Q: News reporter Connie Chung married what daytime television host in 1984?

A: Maury Povich

 Q: Are Yukon Golds a type of jewelry, potato, apple, or orange?

A: Potato

 Q: What sheer netting is typically used to make a bride's veil or ballerina's tutu?

A: Tulle

 Q: What is a double mezzaluna: an ice-skating jump, a creamy sorbet, or an old-fashioned chopping tool?

A: An old-fashioned chopping tool

 Q: Patsy and Edina are the main characters in what British TV show?

A: *Absolutely Fabulous*

Q: What lush shade-loving plant shares its name with a character from *Charlotte's Web*?

A: Fern

Q: Which *View* co-host appeared in a Payless Shoes ad campaign in 2002?

A: Star Jones

Q: Which of these can be found in toothpaste products to help make your teeth whiter: baking powder or baking soda?

A: Baking soda

 Q: What is the fancy French term for comforter?

A: Duvet

 Q: Where would you buy an item from the Angel Collection?

A: Victoria's Secret

 Q: What type of stone do people use to scrape dead skin from their feet?

A: Pumice

37

Q: Which herb, often used for soups, sauces, and Italian cooking, is not usually eaten?

A: Bay leaf

38

Q: What 1850 novel features Hester Prynne as its main character?

A: *The Scarlet Letter* (by Nathaniel Hawthorne)

39

Q: What singer founded Lilith Fair, the all-female music festival, in 1996?

A: Sarah McLachlan

 40

Q: What do you call a sleeveless shirt that fastens behind the neck and back?

A: A halter top

 41

Q: What former Olympic sprinter died from heart seizure in 1998 at the age of 38?

A: Florence Griffith-Joyner (Flo-Jo)

 42

Q: What does alpha hydroxy acid do: whiten teeth, exfoliate skin, or suppress the appetite?

A: Exfoliate skin

Q: What do you call gold-toned powder or cream that is used to create a suntanned look?

A: Bronzer

Q: Which of the following is good for removing gum from hair: peanut butter, vinegar, or Tabasco sauce?

A: Peanut butter

Q: Which of the following is not a magazine for new parents: *BabyTalk*, *Bringing Up Baby*, or *Parenting?*

A: *Bringing Up Baby*

Q: In *The Sound of Music,* what delicate, white flower figured heavily in one song?

A: Edelweiss

Q: In *Bridget Jones's Diary,* does Bridget end up with Daniel Cleaver or Mark Darcy?

A: Mark Darcy

Q: How much is a Susan B. Anthony coin worth?

A: One U.S. dollar

 Q: What is the name of the sexy sleeveless top a woman typically wears underneath her blouse?

A: A camisole

 Q: What product claims that it is "strong enough for a man, but made for a woman"?

A: Secret® (deodorant)

 Q: What American legend, born in 1860, is best known as the nation's finest markswoman?

A: Annie Oakley

Q: Is commercially made buttermilk low or high in fat?

A: Low (It's true!)

Q: What "Man! I Feel Like a Woman" singer married music producer Mutt Lange in 1993?

A: Shania Twain

Q: What gemstone cut has a narrow rectangular shape: a baguette, a brilliant, or a marquise?

A: Baguette

Q: After potting a plant, should you water it immediately or wait at least an hour?

A: Water it immediately.

Q: What does SIDS stand for?

A: Sudden Infant Death Syndrome

Q: What is the name of the handheld tool made to mash fresh garlic cloves?

A: Garlic press

Q: Which one of these is not a color: organdy, cyan, or periwinkle?

A: Organdy (It's a type of sheer fabric.)

Q: What well-known author wrote *Are You There God? It's Me, Margaret.* and *Blubber*?

A: Judy Blume

Q: Which 1970s sex symbol got serious in *Extremities* and *The Burning Bed*?

A: Farrah Fawcett

Q: A paraffin wrap is a treatment one usually gets on what two parts of the body?

A: Hands and feet

Q: Who wrote the book *The Joy Luck Club*?

A: Amy Tan

Q: Which type of wine is *not* white: Chardonnay, Petite Sirah, or Riesling?

A: Petite Sirah

Q: Where did New York Giants hunk Jason Sehorn propose to actress Angie Harmon in 2000?

A: Live on *The Tonight Show with Jay Leno*

Q: In which season would it be most difficult to find tulips: spring, fall, or winter?

A: Fall

Q: What type of pearl is created by the insertion of a grain of sand into an oyster: a freshwater or cultured pearl?

A: A cultured pearl

 Q: What is the common term for rhinoplasty?

A: A nose job

 Q: When coloring eggs, which ingredient is never used: vinegar, water, or oil?

A: Oil

 Q: What did the Germans dub the Soviet Union's three regiments of women fighter pilots formed in 1942: the Wicked Wenches, the Night Witches, or the Dames of Death?

A: The Night Witches

 Q: What Jamaican "Miss" is famed for her psychic hotline?

A: Miss Cleo

 Q: What does TSS stand for?

A: Toxic Shock Syndrome

 Q: What French word meaning "bundle" refers to a bride's honeymoon clothes?

A: Trousseau

Q: What fitness expert is also the author of nine books, including the New York Times bestseller, *Never Say Diet*?

A: Richard Simmons

Q: What is the term used to describe a women's garment that is fitted a few inches above the waist?

A: Empire waist

Q: Jerry Seinfeld's former girlfriend, Shoshana Lonstein, capitalized on her newfound fame with her own line of what in 1998?

A: Lingerie

Q: What sauce is used to make Eggs Benedict?

A: Hollandaise

Q: What rocker played *General Hospital*'s Dr. Noah Blake from 1981–82?

A: Rick Springfield

Q: Redux and what other waist-shrinking drug got yanked from the market by the FDA in the 1990s?

A: Fen-phen

 Q: Peaking in popularity in the early 1980s, are "jellies" a kind of barrette, lip-gloss, or shoe?

A: Shoe

 Q: Who took home the gold in women's figure skating at the 2002 Winter Olympics?

A: Sarah Hughes

Q: What symbol is associated with the Zodiac sign Cancer?

A: Crab

82

Q: What four "somethings" is a bride traditionally supposed to have with her on her wedding day?

A: Something old, something new, something borrowed, something blue

---

83

Q: Name two ingredients found in a basic pesto sauce.

A: Olive oil, basil, garlic, pine nuts, and cheese

84

Q: Who is actress Blythe Danner's famous daughter?

A: Gwyneth Paltrow

85

Q: What is the female equivalent of a Bar Mitzvah?

A: A Bat Mitzvah

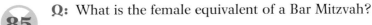

86

Q: What is British TV sensation Jamie Oliver better known as?

A: The Naked Chef

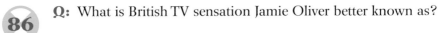

87

Q: What plant is known to soothe a sunburn?

A: Aloe

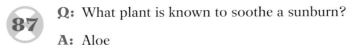

Q: An amethyst comes in shades of what color?

88

A: Purple (violet)

Q: Who wrote the novels *How Stella Got her Groove Back* and *Waiting to Exhale*?

89

A: Terry McMillan

Q: What tribute includes over 37,000 panels and covers over 16 acres?

90

A: The AIDS Quilt

 Q: What is designer Kate Spade most famous for making?

A: Handbags

 Q: Which of the following hand/body lotions comes in deep blue packaging: Nivea, Ponds, or Lubriderm?

A: Nivea

 Q: In a bedroom, where would you find a sham?

A: On a pillow

Q: What 1999 book, written by fashion designer Cynthia Rowley and *New York Times* style editor Ilene Rosenzweig, was billed as a "Girl's Guide to the Good Life"?

A: *Swell*

Q: Pledge®, Old English®, and Behold® are all brands of what?

A: Furniture polish

Q: What 1970s fragrance suggested women could "bring home the bacon, fry it up in a pan, and never let you forget you're a man"?

A: Enjoli

Q: Name the citrus-like oil used in candles that is known as a mosquito repellent.

A: Citronella

Q: Name the doctor of psychology who became an *Oprah Winfrey* regular in 1998.

A: Dr. Phil (McGraw)

Q: What type of tall and slender wineglass is preferred for champagne?

A: A flute

Q: What is the name of the ring given to someone that symbolizes an agreement to become engaged in the future?

A: Promise ring

Q: What is the first line of Gloria Gaynor's "I Will Survive"?

A: "First I was afraid, I was petrified . . ."

Q: What product is the company Hard Candy most famous for making?

A: Nail polish

 103

Q: What were pink Big Wheels for girls originally called?

A: Powder Puffs

 104

Q: What does a yellow rose symbolize: friendship, lust, or purity?

A: Friendship

 105

Q: What is Madonna's daughter's first name?

A: Lourdes

Q: Finish this line from a well-known Shakespearean sonnet: "Shall I compare thee to a ___ ___?"

A: summer's day

Q: Before her acting career took off, which shampoo company did Kim Basinger model for?

A: Breck (She was their "Breck Girl.")

Q: Most airlines forbid a woman to fly after how many weeks into pregnancy: 20–24 weeks, 26–30 weeks, or 34–36 weeks?

A: 34–36 weeks

 Q: Which author wrote the best-selling Three Sisters Island trilogy, which includes *Dance Upon the Air, Heaven and Earth,* and *Face the Fire*?

A: Nora Roberts

 Q: Which fashion designer created the now infamous sequined pointy bras worn by Madonna: Christian Dior, Jean-Paul Gaultier, or Gianni Versace?

A: Jean-Paul Gaultier

 Q: What do you call a semi-circular jeweled headdress?

A: A tiara

Q: Katie Couric and Matt Lauer are co-hosts of what morning TV show?

A: *The Today Show*

Q: Which stemmed glass has a wider bowl: a red or white wine glass?

A: A red wine glass

Q: Are bolero jackets short or long?

A: Short

 115 **Q:** What is the traditional gift for a first wedding anniversary?

A: Paper

---

 116 **Q:** Which daytime talk show host starred as Tracy Turnblad in the 1988 movie *Hairspray*?

A: Ricki Lake

---

117 **Q:** What sturdy shoes typically have a thick wooden heel and are often associated with Northern Europe?

A: Clogs

Q: What is a chanterelle?

A: A wild mushroom

Q: What is a woman's sixth sense?

A: Intuition

Q: What is the name of Oprah Winfrey's production company?

A: Harpo (that's Oprah spelled backwards)

Q: What item found in a medicine cabinet is said to help keep cut flowers fresh?

A: Aspirin

Q: What is the name for the art of trimming trees or shrubs into ornamental shapes?

A: Topiary

Q: Finish this slumber party chant: "Light as a feather,..."

A: "...stiff as a board"

Q: What pattern most resembles gingham: plaid, paisley, or toile?

A: Plaid

Q: Who was India's first female Prime Minister?

A: Indira Gandhi

Q: On the TV series *I Love Lucy,* who were Lucy and Ricky's best friends?

A: Fred and Ethel Mertz

Q: In the 1989 romantic comedy, *Say Anything,* John Cusack's character serenades Ione Skye with what Peter Gabriel song?

A: "In Your Eyes"

Q: How many A's appear in Barbra Streisand's first and last name?

A: Three

Q: What's the name for a low u-shaped neckline on a dress or blouse?

A: Scoop neck

Q: In 2001, who made a guest-appearance on *Friends* as Will—Ross, Rachel, and Monica's former chubby high school chum?

A: Brad Pitt

Q: What type of physical conditioning, brought to the U.S. by its founder and namesake in the 1920s, became fashionable with the fit and famous in the late '90s?

A: Pilates

Q: What mineral is valued as a gem when sky blue in color?

A: Turquoise

Q: Which of the following brands do *not* make baby clothes: OshKosh, Gymboree, or ChildLife?

A: ChildLife (They make backyard play sets.)

Q: What is the name of the politically based and often controversial '70s show starring Bea Arthur?

A: *Maude*

Q: What type of body art, trendy in the late 1990s, comes from an ancient practice and uses a reddish-brown stain that typically fades after six weeks?

A: Henna tattooing

136

Q: What anesthetic shot may a woman receive during childbirth?

A: An epidural

137

Q: What critically acclaimed series debuted in 2001, and features the sassy mother/daughter duo played by Lauren Graham and Alexis Bledel?

A: *The Gilmore Girls*

138

Q: What "family" does a scallion belong to?

A: The onion family

 Q: Which one of these is *not* a flower: hyacinth, freesia, or gabardine?

A: Gabardine (It's a type of fabric.)

 Q: What was the name of the interior design agency on *Designing Women?*

A: Sugarbaker's

 Q: Which manufacturer does *not* make lingerie: La Perla, Natori, or Benefit?

A: Benefit

Q: Where would you find a slipcover?

A: On furniture

Q: On *Bewitched,* what was Samantha's daughter's name?

A: Tabitha

Q: What daytime soap super-couple divorced after twenty years in 2001?

A: *General Hospital*'s Luke and Laura

 Q: Which cosmetic brand includes the hair color line called Natural Instincts: Revlon, Clairol, or L'Oreal?

A: Clairol

 Q: What is the name of the candle that a bride and groom light together during their wedding ceremony?

A: The unity candle

 Q: What fitness program, first popularized in the 1970s, combines aerobic exercise and jazz dancing?

A: Jazzercise®

 Q: Is Michael Kors a famous hairstylist, fashion designer, or gourmet chef?

A: Fashion designer

 Q: What type of beads did teens in the '60s love to sport around their necks as a symbol of friendship?

A: Love beads

 Q: What is the nickname of Molly Ringwald's *Pretty in Pink* sidekick, played by Jon Cryer?

A: Duckie

 Q: What is the name of the rigid supports sewn vertically into a bustier or a corset that help maintain a slim, shapely look about the torso?

A: Stays (or bones)

 Q: As of 2001, how many daytime Emmy®'s has Susan Lucci won?

A: One

 Q: The pump that creates and dispenses a fine spray of perfume is called what: an atomizer, an astringent, or a French brume?

A: An atomizer

Q: Is a chemise a type of scarf, slip, or stocking?

A: Slip

Q: In the 1989 movie *Steel Magnolias,* what were Shelby's wedding colors?

A: Blush and bashful

Q: How many petals does a cinquefoil flower have?

A: Five

Q: What color gown does a debutante typically wear at her coming out ball?

A: White

Q: What classic novel by Frances Hodgson Burnett made it to Broadway in 1991?

A: *The Secret Garden*

Q: Where would you find a huppa?

A: At a Jewish wedding

Q: Does an annual plant bloom just once or once per year?

A: Just once

- - - - - - - - - - - - - - - - -

Q: Name three of the four pop stars who collaborated on a 2001 cover of the 1970s hit "Lady Marmalade."

A: Christina Aguilera, Lil' Kim, Mya, and Pink

- - - - - - - - - - - - - - - - -

Q: A colicky infant is prone to do what: cry, coo, or sleep?

A: Cry

Q: What detective TV series featured television's first female police officer?

A: *The Mod Squad*

Q: Which American icon made the pillbox hat popular in the 1960s?

A: Jacqueline Kennedy

Q: Who wrote *A Room of One's Own*?

A: Virginia Woolf

 Q: What is the main ingredient in baba ganoush?

A: (Pureed) eggplant

 Q: What relaxation therapy uses essential oils to enhance one's well-being?

A: Aromatherapy

 Q: Which fabric is see-through: chenille or chiffon?

A: Chiffon

Q: Base makeup is also referred to as what: concealer, toner, or foundation?

A: Foundation

Q: What former talk show host has a line of clothing sold in Wal-Mart stores?

A: Kathie Lee Gifford

Q: What is the main ingredient in a frittata?

A: Eggs

 Q: What is the married equivalent to the maid of honor called?

A: The matron of honor

- - - - - - - - - - - -

 Q: On the television show, how did Diana change into Wonder Woman?

A: She spun around

- - - - - - - - - - - -

 Q: What bath product claims to "take you away"?

A: Calgon

Q: Who plays Grace on the hit sitcom *Will and Grace*?

A: Debra Messing

Q: In the ribbon event in rhythmic gymnastics, what must the ribbon never do?

A: Touch any part of the gymnast's body

Q: What profession would require the use of an orange stick?

A: Manicurist

178

Q: Who portrayed Mrs. Robinson in the 2002 Broadway debut of *The Graduate*?

A: Kathleen Turner

179

Q: What silver item is sometimes put in the bride's shoe as part of tradition?

A: A sixpence

180

Q: What do you call decorative twisted threads or narrow strips of fabric that hang from the edges of clothing, curtains, or upholstery?

A: Fringe

Q: What skincare brand has featured Martha Quinn, Jennifer Love Hewitt, and Mandy Moore as commercial spokeswomen?

A: Neutrogena®

Q: In layman's terms, what has happened when a pregnant women's amniotic sack has ruptured?

A: Her water has broken

Q: Actress Deidre Hall stars as Dr. Marlena Evans on what daytime soap opera?

A: *Days of Our Lives*

Q: What month is dedicated to National Breast Cancer Awareness?

A: October

Q: Which French chef has hosted a cooking TV show with daughter Claudine?

A: Jacques Pépin

Q: What 1997 Oprah Book Club® selection chronicled the dysfunctional life of Dolores Price?

A: *She's Come Undone*

Q: Which fashion designer took over Gianni Versace's business after his death?

A: Donatella Versace

Q: How many carats is pure gold: 18, 24, or 28?

A: 24 carats

Q: What is Aquanet?

A: Hairspray

Q: What is the name for a tube of fabric (or fur) used to keep hands warm?

A: A muff

Q: What was the name of V.C. Andrews' follow-up to her best-selling 1977 debut, *Flowers in the Attic*?

A: *Petals on the Wind*

Q: What is Spice Girl Emma Bunton's stage name?

A: Baby Spice

 Q: What kind of acid helps prevent birth defects?

A: Folic acid

 Q: What 1973 novel by Erica Jong did Henry Miller trumpet as "a female *Tropic of Cancer*"?

A: *Fear of Flying*

 Q: Who is Xena: Warrior Princess' kick-butt sidekick?

A: Gabrielle (played by Renee O'Connor)

Q: Who played the beautiful Buttercup in the 1987 movie *The Princess Bride*?

A: Robin Wright

Q: What bionic body part does the Bionic Woman have that the Six Million Dollar Man doesn't?

A: A bionic ear (He has a bionic eye.)

Q: Which of these well-known mystery authors murdered a friend's mother, inspiring the film *Heavenly Creatures*: Mary Higgins Clark, Anne Perry, or Agatha Christie?

A: Anne Perry

Q: In 1960, what track and field star became the first American woman to win three gold medals in the Olympics?

199

A: Wilma Rudolph

200

Q: Who played Dorothy Parker in the 1994 movie, *Mrs. Parker and the Vicious Circle*?

A: Jennifer Jason Leigh

201

Q: What famous feminist wrote *Revolution from Within*?

A: Gloria Steinem

Q: In Shakespeare's *Romeo and Juliet,* who dies first: Romeo or Juliet?

A: Romeo

Q: In the 1998 movie *You've Got Mail,* what kind of store did Meg Ryan's character own?

A: A children's bookstore

Q: What magazine publisher puts out *Vogue, Bride's, Vanity Fair,* and *Architectural Digest*?

A: Condé Nast Publications

Q: Who was the subject of the book *Mommie Dearest?*

A: Joan Crawford

Q: In what movie did Oprah Winfrey make her big screen debut in 1985?

A: *The Color Purple*

Q: What's the female portion of a flowering plant called?

A: The pistil

208

Q: What actor shared the 1999 MTV Movie Award for Best Kiss with Gwyneth Paltrow?

A: Joseph Fiennes (for *Shakespeare in Love*)

209

Q: *Dr. Quinn, Medicine Woman* takes place in what western state?

A: Colorado

210

Q: Jemima Puddleduck, Mrs. Tiggywinkle, and the Two Bad Mice are all characters in which author's books?

A: Beatrix Potter

Q: What cosmetics brand uses the tag line "because you're worth it"?

A: L'Oreal

Q: Which Brontë sister wrote *Wuthering Heights:* Emily or Charlotte?

A: Emily Brontë

Q: Do you need a partner to dance the foxtrot?

A: Yes

Q: Which is considered the unhealthier fat: saturated or unsaturated?

A: Saturated fat

Q: What publishing company, founded in 1949, is famous for its romance novels?

A: Harlequin (Enterprises Ltd.)

Q: What daytime talk show host starred in the movie version of *Harriet the Spy*?

A: Rosie O'Donnell

 Q: What nightclub impresario married supermodel Cindy Crawford in 1998?

A: Rande Gerber

 Q: The movie *Coal Miner's Daughter* is a biography of which country music star?

A: Loretta Lynn

 Q: What term refers to the fertilization of an egg in a laboratory?

A: In vitro

220

Q: What superstore features a housewares line from Martha Stewart?

A: Kmart

221

Q: After what 1950s fashion icon is actress Parker Posey rumored to be named?

A: Suzy Parker

222

Q: What Hollywood star filed for divorce from comedian Tom Green in 2001?

A: Drew Barrymore

 Q: According to a best-selling book series, what kind of soup is good for the soul?

A: Chicken soup

 Q: Former Philippines First Lady Imelda Marcos was well known for her collection of what?

A: Shoes

 Q: What actress had a major "make-under" for her role as Lotte in 1999's *Being John Malkovich*?

A: Cameron Diaz

Q: What rising star was shot to death by the president of her own fan club and later portrayed by Jennifer Lopez in a 1997 movie?

A: Selena

Q: In *Little House on the Prairie,* what was the first name of the bratty Oleson girl?

A: Nellie

Q: What French actor starred alongside Andie McDowell in the 1991 romantic comedy *Green Card*?

A: Gérard Depardieu

Q: According to the book *The Rules,* a girl should never date a guy for more than how many years: one, two, or three?

A: Two years

Q: Who is Maria Eva Duarte better known as?

A: Eva Peron

Q: Who is the spunky protagonist in Ludwig Bemelmans' series of children's books, featuring "twelve little girls in two straight lines"?

A: Madeline

Q: Who does Elizabeth Bennet finally marry in Jane Austen's *Pride and Prejudice*?

A: Mr. Darcy

Q: What actor starred with Audrey Hepburn in the romantic comedy *Roman Holiday*?

A: Gregory Peck

Q: What Hollywood diva walked down the aisle with dancer/choreographer Cris Judd in 2001?

A: Jennifer Lopez

235

Q: What animated threesome features Blossom, Buttercup, and Bubbles?

A: The Powerpuff Girls

236

Q: Teen R&B princesses Monica and Brandy collaborated on what 1998 hit?

A: "The Boy is Mine"

237

Q: According to Dr. John Gray, if men are from Mars, where are women from?

A: Venus

Q: Who wrote *I Know Why the Caged Bird Sings*?

A: Maya Angelou

- - - - - - - - - - - - - - - -

Q: In what department of Macy's would you shop for the brand Steve Madden?

A: The shoe department

- - - - - - - - - - - - - - - -

Q: What is the name of Barbie's little sister?

A: Skipper

241

Q: On what weekday, week, and month does Mother's Day fall?

A: The second Sunday of May.

242

Q: What sweet treat is commonly found in ambrosia salad?

A: Marshmallows

243

Q: What sweet-smelling doll, first released in 1979, hung out with fruity friends like Blueberry Muffin, Huckleberry Pie, and Raspberry Tart?

A: Strawberry Shortcake

Q: What glossy magazine, launched in 1983, shares its name with a 19th-century novel by William Makepeace Thackeray?

A: *Vanity Fair*

Q: What whimsical film, released in 2001, features a quixotic young French woman who toys with destiny?

A: *Amélie*

Q: In 1983, who became the first American woman in space?

A: Sally Ride

Q: Faith Hill married what fellow country superstar in 1996?

A: Tim McGraw

Q: Helen Hunt won her first Oscar® for her role as Carol Connelly in what 1997 romantic comedy?

A: *As Good As It Gets*

Q: In what year were U.S. women given the right to vote: 1910, 1920, or 1930?

A: 1920

250

Q: In 1992, what female player became the youngest ever inducted into the Tennis Hall of Fame?

A: Tracy Austin

251

Q: What elegant product is Waterford best known for?

A: Crystal

252

Q: Is platinum or white gold typically more expensive?

A: Platinum

Q: What perennial flowering shrub is closely associated with the Christmas season?

A: The poinsettia

Q: On TV's *Beverly Hills 90210,* which character claimed to have had a nose job?

A: Kelly

Q: Which of these comes from a plant: a wool sweater, blue jeans, or a silk scarf?

A: Blue jeans (the cotton plant)

Q: On what famous ship did American Molly Brown make a name for herself?

A: The *Titanic*

Q: What book by Cameron Tuttle, published in 2000, came with a pink plastic cover and offered girls tips on getting what they want?

A: *The Bad Girl's Guide to Getting What You Want*

Q: What top-selling medicinal herb is said to fight off colds and flu?

A: Echinacea

 Q: What sturdy synthetic fiber did Wallace Carothers create in 1934 that gave Dupont a leg up on the competition?

A: Nylon

 Q: What onetime First Lady is a former fashion model, a feminist, and a recovering alcoholic?

A: Betty Ford

 Q: The mice Bianca and Bernard star in what Disney animated classic?

A: *The Rescuers*

262

Q: What famous fictional Southern belle vowed she'd never be hungry again?

A: Scarlett O'Hara

263

Q: Which young woman won the U.S. Open, the Australian Open, and Wimbledon in 1997—and shares her first name with another tennis great?

A: Martina Hingis

264

Q: Did Geena Davis play Thelma or Louise?

A: Thelma

Q: What is the name of Josie and the Pussycats' cat?

A: Sebastian

Q: What does the HRH in Prince William's title stand for?

A: His Royal Highness

Q: What name is given to the leading ballerina of a ballet company?

A: Prima ballerina

268

Q: What magazine made Beverly Johnson the first African American cover girl of a major fashion publication?

A: *Vogue*

269

Q: Christie's held an auction in 1997 for what royal icon's collection of gowns?

A: Diana, Princess of Wales

270

Q: In *My Fair Lady,* who did Henry Higgins transform into a proper English lady?

A: Eliza Doolittle

Q: What theme song from *The Bodyguard* did Whitney Houston take to number one in 1992?

A: "I Will Always Love You"

Q: What larger relative of a chive sounds like it needs a plumber?

A: A leek

Q: What 19th-century artist painted *Starry Night*?

A: Vincent Van Gogh

Q: What is the name of the high school in the movie *Grease*?

A: Rydell High

- - - - - - - - - - - - - - - -

Q: What is vichyssoise?

A: A cold potato soup

- - - - - - - - - - - - - - - -

Q: What beauty treatment did Cleopatra use on a daily basis?

A: Milk baths

 Q: In 1900, the first female American athlete won an Olympic event. What was *her* sport?

A: Golf (Margaret Abbott)

 Q: What *Dallas* star has her own line of skin care products?

A: Victoria Principal

 Q: What is wicker furniture typically made of?

A: Woven cane or bamboo

Q: What was the first product that Tom's of Maine marketed?

A: Toothpaste

Q: How many standing ballet positions are there?

A: Five

Q: What do you call the inner layer of an oyster shell?

A: Mother-of-pearl

Q: Who is the Roman goddess of love?

A: Venus

Q: What do you call a small flat case containing a mirror, powderpuff, and face powder?

A: Compact

Q: What kind of starch do you use to thicken sauces?

A: Corn starch

Q: What top-selling medicinal herb is said to ward off depression naturally?

A: St. John's Wort

Q: What is the name given to a piece of jewelry worn around the ankle?

A: An anklet

Q: What do the initials RSVP stand for?

A: Respondez-vous s'il vous plait

 289

Q: Traditionally, who pays for the wedding rehearsal dinner?

A: The groom's parents

 290

Q: In which of these gymnastic positions is the gymnast's body perfectly straight: layout, pike, or tuck?

A: Layout

 291

Q: In sewing, what do you call the small metal cap that protects your finger from getting pricked?

A: A thimble

292

Q: In nutrition, what is "The Zone"?

A: A diet plan

293

Q: Is merino a type of wool, silk, or cotton?

A: Wool

294

Q: Name the famous British scientist who went ape observing chimpanzees in their natural habitat.

A: Jane Goodall

295

Q: What ingredient do you put in pastry to make it crumbly?

A: Shortening

296

Q: After the death of her husband and skating partner in 1995, what Russian Olympian went on to perform in women's singles?

A: Ekaterina Gordeeva

297

Q: What do the initials OB/GYN stand for?

A: Obstetrician/gynecologist

Q: What product is "99.44% pure"?

A: Ivory soap

Q: Which health and fitness writer penned the best-selling book *Stop the Insanity*?

A: Susan Powter

Q: Can women get pregnant while they are nursing?

A: Yes

Q: What is shiatsu?

A: A Japanese form of massage

Q: What color does your hair turn if you add henna?

A: Red/auburn

Q: What cosmetics company makes White Linen perfume?

A: Estée Lauder

Q: What country singer urged women to "stand by your man"?

304

A: Tammy Wynette

305

Q: What is a demitasse?

A: A small cup used to serve very strong black coffee

306

Q: Bela Karoli is considered the most successful coach in the history of what sport?

A: Women's gymnastics

307

Q: Bess and George (Georgia) are the loyal sidekicks of what fictional teen sleuth?

A: Nancy Drew

308

Q: What would you use an emery board for?

A: To file your nails

309

Q: What is the name of the church where Prince Charles and Lady Diana exchanged wedding vows?

A: St. Paul's Cathedral

Q: Which Nobel prize-winning author wrote *Beloved* and *Paradise*?

A: Toni Morrison

Q: What is a chignon: a French dessert, a hairstyle, or a type of scarf?

A: A hairstyle

Q: Slices of what green vegetable can be put on the eyes to reduce swelling?

A: Cucumber

 Q: What is the meat in coq au vin?

A: Chicken

 Q: What was the theme song for the movie *Ghost*?

A: "Unchained Melody"

 Q: How many ovaries does a woman have?

A: Two

Q: How many husbands did Marilyn Monroe have?

A: Three (Jim Dougherty, Joe DiMaggio, Arthur Miller)

Q: Who wrote the novel *Frankenstein*?

A: Mary Shelley

Q: What sweet-smelling flower shares its name with a character from Disney's *Aladdin*?

A: Jasmine

Q: What 19th-century sharpshooter preferred to wear pants?

A: Calamity Jane (Martha Jane Bourke)

Q: What herb is a natural breath freshener?

A: Parsley

Q: What do you call a necklace that's worn snugly around the neck?

A: A choker

Q: Who was the first female Prime Minister of Pakistan?

A: Benazir Bhutto

Q: In 1994, the U.S. Figure Skating Association banned which skater for life?

A: Tonya Harding

Q: What 1988 tearjerker starred Bette Midler and Barbara Hershey?

A: *Beaches*

 Q: What heats an Easy Bake Oven?

A: A light bulb

 Q: When a baby is born breech, how does it exit the birth canal?

A: Feet or buttocks first

 Q: What 1995 animated film featured the Oscar® and Grammy®-winning song, "Colors of the Wind"?

A: *Pocahontas*

Q: From what animal does cashmere wool come?

A: Goat

Q: Which type of nut is used to make marzipan?

A: Almonds

Q: What Renaissance man painted the celebrated 16th century portrait of Francesco del Giocondo's wife?

A: Leonardo da Vinci (*The Mona Lisa*)

 331

Q: What do you call the ancient Chinese approach to interior decorating?

A: Feng shui

 332

Q: A top-loading bobbin and deep feed are features you would find on a what?

A: Sewing machine

 333

Q: What product boasts that it "has wings"?

A: Always® Maxi Pads

Q: What disease, most commonly found in women, causes the bones to weaken and thin?

A: Osteoporosis

Q: Who holds the record for most Wimbledon women's titles?

A: Billie Jean King (20)

Q: What cocktail's ingredients are vodka, cranberry juice, lime juice, and triple sec?

A: A cosmopolitan

Q: Name the lead singer of the all-girl band The Go-Go's.

A: Belinda Carlisle

Q: What length are capri pants?

A: Below the knees and above the ankles

Q: What 14-year-old girl achieved a perfect score in gymnastics at the 1976 Olympics?

A: Nadia Comaneci

Q: Hayley Mills played twin sisters of divorced parents in the original version of what 1960s film?

A: *The Parent Trap*

Q: What youthful national heroine led the French army to victory at the Siege of Orléans in 1429?

A: Joan of Arc

Q: What energy bar is made especially for women?

A: Luna Bar®

Q: Is Polly Pockets a financial guru, a toy, or a clothing company?

A: A toy

Q: What do you call the long back section of a dress that trails along the floor?

A: The train

Q: What contains more fat: a tablespoon of peanut butter or two slices of bacon?

A: A tablespoon of peanut butter

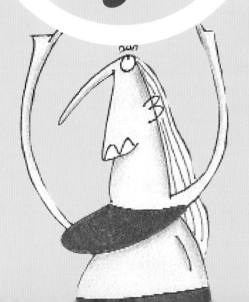

Q: What action figure, first introduced in 1972, rode the Stunt Cycle?

A: Evel Knievel

Q: If you're in the privy, where are you?

A: In the outhouse (or latrine)

Q: What comedian and former *SNL* star signed on to co-host *Monday Night Football* in 2000?

A: Dennis Miller

Q: Who landed the coveted *Sports Illustrated* swimsuit edition cover in 2002: Yamila Diaz-Rahi, Heidi Klum, or Josie Maran?

A: Yamila Diaz-Rahi

Q: What's the tasty term for files that track your online surfing habits?

A: Cookies

Q: What are the official Cub Scout colors?

A: Blue and gold

 Q: What legendary sports broadcaster, famed for saying "Holy Cow!," died in 1998?

A: Harry Caray

 Q: Is a clay pigeon a pigeon lure, a shooting target, or a prison informant?

A: A shooting target

 Q: What do you call a wrench with adjustable jaws?

A: A monkey wrench

 10

Q: What is the name of Conan O'Brien's former co-host on *The Late Show*?

A: Andy Richter

 11

Q: In what game are "spinning" and "jarring" illegal moves: foosball, darts, or ice hockey?

A: Foosball

 12

Q: On average, which fish grows larger: a perch or a trout?

A: A trout

Q: What baseball team was featured in the movie *Major League*?

A: The Cleveland Indians

Q: Aside from the rock band, what does K.I.S.S. stand for?

A: Keep it simple, stupid.

Q: What notorious American outlaw led a gang of bank and train robbers in the late 1800s with his brother Frank?

A: Jesse James

Q: In weightlifting, what muscles do you have to work to get "big guns"?

A: Your biceps

Q: Who stars as Jackie Chan's sidekick in the *Rush Hour* movies?

A: Chris Tucker

Q: What major car company uses a prancing horse as its trademark?

A: Ferrari

Q: In *The Godfather,* who were Don Vito Corleone's three sons?

A: Michael, Fredo (Frederico), and Sonny (Santino)

Q: What band released "Heart-Shaped Box" in 1993?

A: Nirvana

Q: What is the usual number of rounds in a heavyweight boxing championship: 10, 12, or 15?

A: 12

Q: In Morse Code, what does a series of three dots, followed by a space and three dashes, followed by a space and three dots translate to?

A: S.O.S.

Q: What weekly PBS TV show features old homes in need of renovation?

A: *This Old House*

Q: What American sporting event was interrupted by an earthquake in 1989?

A: The World Series

 Q: What band is fronted by singer Scott Stapp?

A: Creed

 Q: As of spring 2002, what is the latest Boeing aircraft model manufactured?

A: 777

 Q: What does a mason do for a living?

A: Lays bricks

 Q: Where might you catch someone spelunking: a cave, an airport, or an oil well?

A: A cave

 Q: What does a dipstick measure?

A: A car's oil level

 Q: Who played Carl Spackler in the 1980 comedy *Caddyshack*?

A: Bill Murray

Q: In *The Outsiders*, what are the names of the two rival gangs?

A: The Greasers and the Socs (short for "social")

Q: What '80s teen pop princess posed for *Playboy* in 2002?

A: Tiffany

Q: What "hottest ride in town" gave Big Wheel® a run for its money when it debuted in 1975?

A: The Green Machine

Q: What British-born singer backs up Eminem on "Stan"?

A: Dido

Q: Who said, " 'Twas a woman who drove me to drink, and I never had the courtesy to thank her for it"?

A: W. C. Fields

Q: What action figure made a comeback in the '80s as a "Real American Hero"?

A: G.I. Joe®

Q: What's a double fisherman?

A: A knot

Q: What is the name of the Simpson's family dog?

A: Santa's Little Helper

Q: Which is longer: a barbell or a dumbbell?

A: A barbell

Q: When grilling a piece of meat that is about two inches thick, should one use high or low heat?

A: High heat

Q: What is the name of Tom Sawyer's girlfriend in Mark Twain's *The Adventures of Tom Sawyer*?

A: Becky Thatcher

Q: During which of these years did the Wright Brothers make history with the first manned plane flight: 1903, 1913, or 1933?

A: 1903

 Q: If a guy is sharing his Copenhagen, what is he sharing?

A: His snuff or chewing tobacco

 Q: What Alaskan mountain, with peaks over 19,000 feet, has the highest summit in North America?

A: Denali (Mount McKinley)

 Q: What 1979 war movie is based on Joseph Conrad's *Heart of Darkness*?

A: *Apocalypse Now*

 Q: The vitamin Biotin is typically taken by men to prevent what?

A: Hair loss

 Q: What automaker manufactures the Carrera and the Boxter?

A: Porsche

 Q: What direction is 180 degrees on a compass?

A: South

 Q: Formerly known as "The Body," Minnesota Governor Jesse Ventura now refers to himself as what?

A: The Mind

 Q: Who plays Reggie Dunlop in the 1977 movie *Slap Shot?*

A: Paul Newman

 Q: Tablas, Zarbs, and Madals are all types of what musical instrument?

A: Drum

Q: What company drove into the die-cast toy car market in 1968?

A: Hot Wheels®

Q: Punch, Macanudo, and Partagas are all brands of what?

A: Cigars

Q: Where would a man wear an ascot: around his neck, around his waist, or on his head?

A: Around his neck (An ascot is a men's scarf that loops under the chin.)

Q: In Dungeons and Dragons, what title was given to the player who narrated the game and kept all the secret maps?

A: The Dungeon Master

Q: What does AWOL stand for?

A: Absent without leave

Q: What athlete titled his 1996 autobiography *Bad as I Wanna Be*?

A: Dennis Rodman

Q: What do you call a hammer with a large rubber head?

A: A rubber mallet

Q: What is Dr. Zog's Sex Wax?

A: A brand of surfboard wax

Q: What game are you playing when you play 301?

A: Darts

 Q: How many fingers are used in the Boy Scouts of America salute?

A: Three

 Q: Did the late Keith Moon play the drums for The Who, Led Zeppelin, or The Rolling Stones?

A: The Who

 Q: What kind of creature does Aqua Man ride?

A: A seahorse

Q: When learning to tandem skydive, is the instructor or the student typically on top?

A: The instructor

Q: Dennis Hopper plays Wyatt/Captain America in what 1969 movie?

A: *Easy Rider*

Q: What veteran TV funnyman played Dorf, the stubby sports buff, in a series of comedy sketches?

A: Tim Conway

 Q: What bicycle manufacturer made the Sting-Ray®?

A: Schwinn

 Q: What football team won Super Bowl XXXVI on Feb. 3, 2002, for the first time in the history of its franchise?

A: The New England Patriots

 Q: If a carpenter says a wall is plumb, does that mean the wall is bumpy, bowed, or vertical?

A: Vertical

 Q: If you're abseiling, what are you doing?

A: Rappeling

 Q: What does YMCA stand for?

A: Young Men's Christian Association

 Q: In the U.S. Marines, how many silver stars does a general have on his/her uniform?

A: Four

Q: What do the Softail, Sportster, and Dyna Glide have in common?

A: They are all Harley-Davidson® motorcycles.

Q: Who starred in *Missing in Action* and *The Delta Force*?

A: Chuck Norris

Q: What is Barbasol®?

A: A brand of shaving products

Q: Name the three original Rolling Stones.

A: Mick Jagger, Keith Richards, and Brian Jones

Q: What does BMW stand for?

A: Bavarian Motor Works

Q: What 2001 film featured characters such as Proximo, Commodus, and Maximus?

A: *Gladiator*

 Q: Which professional sport is the World Cup?

A: Soccer

 Q: From what part of a cow does a top round steak come?

A: The leg

 Q: What product (nicknamed the NES) was the number one selling toy in America in 1987?

A: The Nintendo Entertainment System

 Q: Name three of the four Marx Brothers.

A: Groucho, Harpo, Chico, and Zeppo

- - - - - - - - - - - - - - - - - - -

 Q: Do Atlantic salmon live in saltwater, freshwater, or both?

A: Both

- - - - - - - - - - - - - - - - - - -

 Q: Where is a clutch located on a motorcycle?

A: On the left handlebar

Q: What vegetable is vodka typically made from?

A: Potatoes

- - - - - - - - - - - - - - - -

Q: How much is a giga: a million, a billion, or a trillion?

A: A billion

- - - - - - - - - - - - - - - -

Q: What living creatures were affectionately dubbed Sea Monkeys and raised by millions of kids in the 1970s?

A: Brine shrimp (or Artemia salina)

Q: What sport does Nick Faldo play?

A: Golf

Q: Who is the main character in the video game (and movie) *Tomb Raider*?

A: Lara Croft

Q: What do you call the froth on top of a glass of beer?

A: The head

Q: What aftershave features an old-fashioned sailing ship as its logo?

A: Old Spice

Q: What is the name of Jimmy Buffet's small restaurant chain, located primarily in the American South?

A: Margaritaville

Q: What year did *Maxim* magazine first hit stands in the United States: 1977, 1987, or 1997?

A: 1997

 Q: What sport has a penalty called face-masking?

A: Football

 Q: Who was *not* a member of the Rat Pack: Dean Martin, Joey Bishop, or Bing Crosby?

A: Bing Crosby

 Q: What sci-fi and fantasy author wrote the classic story *Something Wicked This Way Comes*?

A: Ray Bradbury

Q: A mason uses a vibrator to remove what from concrete?

A: Air pockets

Q: On a vehicle, what does RPM stand for?

A: Revolutions per minute

Q: Not counting the cue ball, how many balls are used in a game of eightball?

A: Fifteen

 Q: What humor columnist wrote the *Complete Guide to Guys*?

A: Dave Barry

—————————————————————

 Q: What adventure sport allegedly started in the jungles of the Vanuatu Islands in the Pacific Ocean?

A: Bungee jumping

—————————————————————

 Q: What disaster-ridden "super" stuntman does Bob Einstein play?

A: Super Dave Osborne

Q: How many wheels would you find on a single trailer semi-truck?

A: Eighteen

Q: What series of reference books take a no-nonsense approach to how-to subjects like technology, taxes, and cooking?

A: ...*For Dummies*

Q: What does the "Five-O" represent in the TV series *Hawaii Five-O*?

A: A special unit of the Hawaii police department

Q: What is a Smith & Wesson Mini-Swat: a pocketknife, a pistol, or hi-tech flytrap?

A: A pocketknife

Q: What name did Guns N' Roses' lead guitarist go by?

A: Slash

Q: What golf tournament was Kevin Costner trying to qualify for in the 1996 movie *Tin Cup*?

A: The U.S. Open

Q: What does *GQ* stand for?

A: *Gentlemen's Quarterly*

Q: What is the natural resource that scientists were looking for on the island in the remake of *King Kong*?

A: Oil

Q: What animal is on the label of a bottle of Schlitz malt liquor?

A: A bull

Q: What is the Iditarod?

A: A dogsled race held every year in Alaska

Q: If you're using the Napoleon method, what are you measuring?

A: Width

Q: What landmark is located under the North Star?

A: The North Pole

Q: What is used to make the shell of classic Airstream camper trailers?

A: Aluminum

Q: What name is on Muhammad Ali's birth certificate?

A: Cassius Clay

Q: What family of toys did robot warriors Raydeen, Dragun, and The Great Mazinga belong to?

A: Shogun Warriors

Q: What type of tool is a ball-peen?

A: Hammer

_____

Q: What does the tree-felling method measure?

A: Height

_____

Q: What kind of equipment does the company John Deere make?

A: Farm equipment

Q: Is Ren of *Ren and Stimpy* a cat, a dog, or a mouse?

A: A dog

Q: What cyclist won the 1999 Tour de France—and set a world record for speed—only two years after winning his battle with testicular cancer?

A: Lance Armstrong

Q: In the world of architecture, what does C.A.D. stand for?

A: Computer-aided design

 Q: What are the names of the original three stooges?

A: Larry, Moe, and Curly

 Q: Isaac Asimov is known for writing novels in what literary genre?

A: Science fiction

 Q: What are the military phonetic letters for A, B, and C?

A: Alpha, Bravo, and Charlie

 Q: What color is the positive terminal on most car batteries?

A: Red

 Q: Is Gorp a type of fish, trail mix, or a hydrophobic fabric?

A: Trail mix

 Q: Which type of cooking device provides the highest heat: a charcoal grill, a broiler, or a gas grill?

A: A charcoal grill

Q: What "Great One" made #99 famous in the National Hockey League?

A: Wayne Gretzky

Q: How many ounces are in a standard can of beer?

A: Twelve

Q: What band did singer Sebastian Bach front?

A: Skid Row

Q: What is the first rank in the Boy Scouts?

A: Tenderfoot

Q: Do cars that get above-average gas mileage generally have more or fewer cylinders than cars that get poor gas mileage?

A: Fewer

Q: How many Air Force One planes are there?

A: Two

Q: Who plays Obi-Wan Kenobi in *Star Wars: Episode I—The Phantom Menace*?

A: Ewan McGregor

Q: What's the name for the gigantic LED displays, often seen at sporting events?

A: Jumbotron®

Q: In baseball, what does it mean if a pitcher is a "southpaw"?

A: The pitcher is left-handed.

Q: In the 1986 movie *The Fly*, who plays Seth, the scientist who invents a teleportation device?

A: Jeff Goldblum

- - - - - - - - - - - - - - - -

Q: When referring to bonds, what goes down when prices go up: stocks, yields, or capital gains?

A: Yields

- - - - - - - - - - - - - - - -

Q: What is the Boy Scouts' motto?

A: Be Prepared

Q: In chess, a rook is also called what?

A: A castle

Q: In golf, what does the term albatross mean?

A: Three under par (or double eagle)

Q: In the stock market, does a bull market refer to a long-term uptrend or downtrend?

A: Uptrend

 Q: What two kinds of alcohol do you mix to make a boiler-maker?

A: Beer and whiskey

 Q: What precious stone is sometimes used in drill bits?

A: Diamond

 Q: What professional basketball player appears in Bruce Lee's last film, *Game of Death*, released in 1978?

A: Kareem Abdul-Jabbar

Q: In 1982, Michael Jordan led which southern school to the NCAA basketball title: University of North Carolina, North Carolina State, or Duke?

A: University of North Carolina

Q: What Academy Award®-winning actress played a Bond Girl in 1983's *Never Say Never Again*?

A: Kim Basinger

Q: How many meters in length is an Olympic-size swimming pool: 25, 50, or 75?

A: 50

 Q: In *Batman*, who is Bruce Wayne's butler?

A: Alfred

 Q: Who did *not* appear in the 1975 musical *Tommy:* Elton John, Tina Turner, Eric Clapton, or Peter Frampton?

A: Peter Frampton

 Q: What sporting event holds the most places among the 30 all-time most-watched TV programs (ranked by total households viewing)?

A: The Super Bowl

Q: What is the championship trophy in professional hockey called?

A: The Stanley Cup

Q: In the late-80s gangster/cop drama *Colors,* starring Sean Penn, what were the two rival gangs' primary colors?

A: Red and blue

Q: In *Star Wars,* what are C3PO and R2D2?

A: Droids

Q: In the original arcade version of *Asteroids,* the control panel options were rotate left, rotate right, fire, thrust, and what?

A: Hyperspace

Q: What's another name for boxing practice using light punches?

A: Sparring

Q: Before he became an actor, Jason Lee (of *Almost Famous, Chasing Amy,* and *Mall Rats*) was a professional in which sport: tennis, skateboarding, or soccer?

A: Skateboarding

Q: In what country is Carlsberg Beer brewed?

A: Denmark

Q: What Hollywood legend starred as Sam Spade in the 1941 film *The Maltese Falcon*?

A: Humphrey Bogart

Q: What classic TV sitcom featured Sergeant Carter, Colonel Klink, and Corporal Newkirk?

A: *Hogan's Heroes*

Q: "Redrum" is murder spelled backwards. Which author made redrum famous?

A: Stephen King

Q: What is the newfangled name of the lead character in the movie *The Matrix*?

A: Neo

Q: In camping, what is an Iodine tablet commonly used for?

A: To purify water for drinking

Q: If you're a "grease monkey," what are you?

A: A mechanic

Q: Name three of the five members of the music group The Traveling Wilburys.

A: Tom Petty, Bob Dylan, Roy Orbison, Jeff Lynne, and George Harrison

---

Q: During which 20th-century war does John Knowles' 1959 classic, *A Separate Peace,* take place?

A: World War II

Q: What character did John Belushi play in the 1978 comedy *Animal House*?

A: Bluto (John "Bluto" Blutarsky)

Q: Are bloaters, ruffes, and walleyes all types of volleyball hits, fish, or frogs?

A: Fish

Q: What New England state is the home of Mark Twain's "Yankee" who took a trip to "King Arthur's Court"?

A: Connecticut (*A Connecticut Yankee in King Arthur's Court*)

Q: What plant is rum made from?

A: Sugar cane

Q: What metals make up solder?

A: Lead and tin

Q: What were the names of the two *Saturday Night Live* bodybuilder characters that wanted to "Pump you up!" in the 1980s?

A: Hans and Franz

Q: What does NASCAR stand for?

A: National Association for Stock Car Auto Racing

Q: What 1970s sitcom featured Detective Stanley Wojciehowicz, Detective Nick Yemana, and Detective Ron Harris?

A: *Barney Miller*

Q: What 1952 classic novel features the character Bilbo Baggins?

A: *The Hobbit*

♀

Q: Tough guy Arnold Schwarzenegger plays a cyborg sent from the future to end lives in what 1984 movie?

A: *The Terminator*

Q: What's the purpose of a muffler on a car?

A: It reduces the noise from car exhaust.

Q: What actor plays Indiana Jones' father in the film *Indiana Jones and the Last Crusade*?

A: Sean Connery

 Q: Who wrote the runaway best sellers *A Time to Kill* and *The Pelican Brief*?

A: John Grisham

 Q: Which is *not* slang for steroids: juice, sauce, milk, or roids?

A: Milk

 Q: In what 1977 movie did Richard Dreyfuss play with his mashed potatoes?

A: *Close Encounters of the Third Kind*

Q: Before Phil Collins stepped up to the mike, who sang lead for Genesis: David Byrne, Peter Gabriel, or Mark Knopfler?

A: Peter Gabriel

Q: During what decade did Robert Moog invent the electric synthesizer?

A: The 1960s

Q: In landscaping, milky spore, neem, and pyrethins are all used for what?

A: Pest control

 Q: What Irish rock group shares its name with a U.S. spy plane?

A: U2

 Q: What type of short poem consists of five lines and shares its name with an Irish county?

A: Limerick

 Q: In a game of pool, which balls are the low numbers: solids or stripes?

A: Solids

Q: What 1978 holiday flick treated viewers to a knife-wielding killer named Michael Myers?

A: *Halloween*

───────────────────

Q: Elvis Presley and Jerry Lee Lewis sang for a record company named for a member of our solar system. Name that company.

A: Sun Records

───────────────────

Q: What chess piece is the only one that doesn't move in a straight line?

A: The knight (horse)

Q: Pump action, cabinet, and ratchet are all types of what tool?

A: Screwdrivers

Q: What controversial rapper's real name is Marshall Mathers?

A: Eminem

Q: The title of the book and television mini-series *Band of Brothers* is taken from a line from what Shakespeare work?

A: *Henry V*

Q: What are the colors of a can of Budweiser beer?

A: Red, white, and blue

Q: True or false: *The X-Men* only include mutant men.

A: False

Q: What long-running TV series aired from 1955–1975, and featured Doc Adams, Miss Kitty, and Marshal Dillon?

A: *Gunsmoke*

 Q: What dark poem by Edgar Allen Poe starts out, "Once upon a midnight dreary..."?

A: "The Raven"

— — — — — — — — — — — — — —

 Q: Who sang lead vocals when Van Halen launched in 1974: Gary Cheron, Sammy Hagar, or David Lee Roth?

A: David Lee Roth

— — — — — — — — — — — — — —

 Q: Does a half-ton pickup truck weigh more than, less than, or exactly half a ton?

A: More than

Q: What does a white diamond-shaped buoy with a cross inside of it signal: proceed with caution, keep out, or stay to the left?

A: Keep out

Q: Knobber, hummle, brocket, and switch are all terms for what type of animal?

A: Deer

Q: What color poker chip is usually assigned the lowest value?

A: White

Q: On *The Dukes of Hazzard,* what was the name of the Dukes' short-shorts wearing cousin?

A: Daisy Duke

Q: What rock band rocked the charts with "In the End" in 2001?

A: Linkin Park

Q: What product comes from "the oldest registered distillery in the United States"?

A: Jack Daniels bourbon

 Q: What liquor is used to make a Mint Julep?

A: Bourbon

 Q: A mason uses a bull float to level what?

A: Concrete

 Q: Which *South Park* character is seriously injured in every episode: Cartman, Chef, or Kenny?

A: Kenny

 Q: Which of King Arthur's knights actually saw the Holy Grail?

A: Percival

 Q: Which U.S. general left the Philippines in World War II and vowed, "I shall return"?

A: General Douglas MacArthur

 Q: What character did Christina Applegate portray on TV's *Married With Children*?

A: Kelly (Bundy)

Q: What laid-back game, created by Mike Marshall, first kicked off in 1972?

A: Hacky Sack

Q: When a carpenter "rips" a piece of wood, is s/he cutting parallel or perpendicular to the grain pattern?

A: Parallel

Q: Tom Wolfe turned a bus tour across the U.S. with Ken Kesey and his Merry Pranksters into what popular book published in the 1960s?

A: *The Electric Kool-Aid Acid Test*

 Q: What do you store in a humidor?

A: Cigars

 Q: Which of these fish is prized for its eggs (a.k.a. caviar): yellow perch, lake sturgeon, or rainbow smelt?

A: Lake sturgeon

 Q: In what city did the St. Louis Rams get their start?

A: Cleveland (then Los Angeles, then St. Louis)

Q: What New York City landmark did Donald Trump put up for sale in March of 2002?

A: The Empire State Building

Q: What Pink Floyd song features the sound of a cash register in the background?

A: "Money" (from 1973's *Dark Side of the Moon*)

Q: Is a hull the back of the boat, structural body of the boat, or the bottom of the boat?

A: Structural body of the boat

Q: In the early 1980s arcade game of the same name, what color is Q*bert?

A: Orange

- - - - - - - - - - - - - - -

Q: Is Neil Peart a famous tennis player, drummer, or football player?

A: Drummer (for the band RUSH)

- - - - - - - - - - - - - - -

Q: What team did the New York Yankees beat to take home their 26th World Series Championship in 2000?

A: The New York Mets

Q: In camping, what is a bowline?

A: A knot

- - - - - - - - - - - - - - - - - -

Q: What band does Heather Locklear's husband, Richie Sambora, play for?

A: Bon Jovi

- - - - - - - - - - - - - - - - - -

Q: Who plays shortstop for Charlie Brown's baseball team?

A: Snoopy

 Q: What company does Tom Hanks work for in the film *Castaway*?

A: FedEx

 Q: What 1990s rapper was born Robert Van Winkle?

A: Vanilla Ice

 Q: What is the top-selling motor oil in the United States?

A: Pennzoil

Q: What's a Havana?

A: A top quality cigar

Q: In the 1987 film *Wall Street*, what character did Michael Douglas play?

A: Gordon Gekko

Q: In carpentry, "level" is the condition that exists when a surface is at what: true horizontal or true vertical?

A: True horizontal

 Q: A gas grill can generate interior heat of approximately what temperature: 400, 600, or 800 degrees?

A: 800 degrees

 Q: In pro football, when a team completes a successful field goal without a touchdown, how many points are scored?

A: Three

 Q: In what year was the table game Air Hockey invented: 1962, 1972, or 1982?

A: 1972

 Q: In Herman Melville's classic novel, what captain unrelentingly pursues Moby Dick, the great white whale?

A: Captain Ahab

 Q: Which actress played Lisa, the computer-made ideal woman, in the movie *Weird Science*?

A: Kelly LeBrock

 Q: What does hi-fi stand for?

A: High fidelity

 Q: In the *Star Trek* series, Mr. Spock is half human and half what?

A: Vulcan

 Q: What legendary rock band composed "Black Dog," "Tangerine," and "Whole Lotta Love"?

A: Led Zeppelin

 Q: What Emmy award-winning PBS TV series is named after a celestial object?

A: *Nova*

Q: In the original *Jurassic Park,* what species of dinosaur devours Donald, the lawyer, while he's in the outhouse?

A: *Tyrannosaurus Rex*

Q: Which gasoline pump has the thinner nozzle: leaded or unleaded?

A: Unleaded

Q: What is the name of the bolt used to fasten a car wheel?

A: A lug bolt

 Q: What is the first name of Tim "The Toolman" Taylor's sidekick and handyman on the TV show *Home Improvement*?

A: Al (Borland)

 Q: In what city and state is Fenway Park located?

A: Boston, Massachusetts

 Q: In what 1955 novel do a group of boys stranded on an island learn a lot about human nature?

A: *Lord of the Flies*

Q: In blackjack, what is an ace worth?

A: One or eleven

Q: On a cigar, where do you typically find the brand name printed?

A: On the band

Q: In computer lingo, what does ISP stand for?

A: Internet service provider

Q: Which type of beer is lighter in color: pilsner or dunkel?

A: Pilsner

Q: Who played keyboard for The Doors: Ray Manzarek, Robby Krieger, or John Densmore?

A: Ray Manzarek

Q: What best-selling book, first published in 1998, is a cheesy parable about change?

A: *Who Moved My Cheese?*

Q: In men's fashion, band, laydown, and wing are all types of what?

A: Shirt collars

Q: What is the highest Celsius temperature at which water freezes?

A: 0° Celsius

Q: What superhero did Peter Parker become after he was bitten by a radioactive spider?

A: Spider-Man

 Q: What do you call a plant that sheds its leaves annually?

A: Deciduous

 Q: In a traditional game of Chinese Checkers, up to how many people can play?

A: Six

 Q: Which actor played boxer Jake La Motta in the movie *Raging Bull*?

A: Robert De Niro

Q: Which galaxy shares its name with a virus strain in a science-fiction thriller by Michael Crichton?

A: Andromeda

Q: What family heirloom was passed down to Bruce Willis's character in the movie *Pulp Fiction*?

A: A watch

Q: In what month is Father's Day?

A: June

Q: What band, whose sounds were first heard in the 1970s, named themselves after elements?

A: Earth, Wind & Fire

Q: What rocker released *Whiplash Smile* in 1986?

A: Billy Idol

Q: What character does Jim Carrey play in *Dumb and Dumber*?

A: Lloyd Christmas

Q: In billiards, what's a scratch?

A: Sinking the cue ball

Q: What "lodge" did Ralph and Ed belong to on *The Honeymooners*?

A: The Raccoon Lodge

Q: Which can go faster: a dragster, a stock car, or an Indy?

A: A dragster

 Q: What is the first name of Dr. Evil's son in *Austin Powers: The Spy Who Shagged Me*?

A: Scott

 Q: What *Baywatch* babe was the "Tool Time" girl on *Home Improvement* from 1991–92?

A: Pamela Anderson

 Q: What does an odometer do?

A: Measures how far a vehicle has traveled.

Q: What war does Tim O'Brien chronicle in his 1990 book, *The Things They Carried*?

A: Vietnam

Q: What is the name of a vehicle that rides on a cushion of air over any flat surface, including water?

A: Hovercraft

Q: Which video game company manufactures *Game Boy* and *Virtual Boy*?

A: Nintendo

Q: Panels made from compressed wood chips and glue are called what: drywall, sheetrock, or particleboard?

A: Particleboard

- - - - - - - - - - - - - - - -

Q: In what city and state could you see Barry Bonds play at PacBell Park?

A: San Francisco, California

- - - - - - - - - - - - - - - -

Q: What almost always has a water pump: a car engine or a toilet?

A: A car engine

Q: Who is Jerry's postman neighbor on the TV series *Seinfeld*?

A: Newman

Q: What media mogul took home the prestigious America's Cup in 1977, skippering the yacht, *Outrageous*?

A: Ted Turner

Q: In what sport do contestants battle to win the Ryder Cup: golf, tennis, or tractor pulls?

A: Golf

Q: What Comedy Central show suggests viewers should "Grab a beer and drop your pants, send the wife and kid to France..."

A: *The Man Show*

Q: The Buffalo Bills played in four consecutive Super Bowls. How many did they win?

A: None

Q: Who wrote *Iron John: A Book About Men*?

A: Robert Bly

 Q: What sort of fighter plane did Tom Cruise fly in the movie *Top Gun*?

A: Tomcat (F-14)

 Q: Who is the lead singer for the band Limp Bizkit?

A: Fred Durst

 Q: What are the three sports in a triathlon?

A: Swimming, bicycling, and running

Q: What feature on your lawn mower cuts the grass into fine pieces and helps fertilize your lawn?

A: Mulcher

Q: What does the 007 in James Bond's title signify?

A: Licensed to kill

Q: According to the official rules of table tennis, a player must win by how many points: one, two, or three?

A: Two

 Q: What are the two events in a winter Olympic biathlon?

A: Cross country skiing and rifle shooting

 Q: Adam Carolla hosts what popular radio show with Dr. Drew Pinsky?

A: "Loveline"

 Q: What does SUV stand for?

A: Sport utility vehicle

Q: Name the character Al Pacino played in *Scarface*.

A: Tony Montana

Q: What type of amphibian leapt to fame in Mark Twain's story set in Calaveras County, California?

A: A frog

Q: To compete as a boxing heavyweight, you must tip the scales at what weight or above?

A: 190 lbs

Q: What car company makes the Explorer?

A: Ford

Q: What is the rhyming name of a pre-game strategy session?

A: Chalk talk

Q: On what cable TV network can you watch *The Crocodile Hunter*?

A: Animal Planet

 Q: What is the largest possible number of points on a single play in NBA basketball?

A: Four (a three point shot plus a free throw)

 Q: Who played the Joker on the *Batman* television series?

A: Cesar Romero

 Q: In which Olympic sport might you see a Daffy, a Zudnik, or a Backscratcher?

A: Freestyle Skiing

Q: Where was the TV series *Nash Bridges* set?

A: San Francisco

———————————————————

Q: What sailing term shares its name with a bulletin board item?

A: Tack

———————————————————

Q: What 1970s musician could play the electric guitar with his teeth?

A: Jimi Hendrix

Q: Who was the first Westerner to climb Mount Everest in 1953?

A: Sir Edmund Hillary

Q: Name the female volleyball player and model who has hosted TV shows such as *The Extremist* and *MTV Sports*?

A: Gabrielle Reece

Q: If your mechanic uses the term "R & I," what does s/he mean?

A: Remove and install

Q: In the movie *National Lampoon's Vacation,* where was Clarke Griswold taking his family?

A: Wally World

Q: What kind of product is Big League Chew®?

A: Bubble gum

Q: The NFL and the AFL merged in what year: 1960, 1970, or 1980?

A: 1970

Q: What was the official ceremony where a squire became a knight called?

A: Dubbing

Q: Helpful John Stockton holds the NBA record for what, with 12,713 in his career?

A: Assists

Q: In carpentry, a dovetail, keyhole, and bow are all types of what?

A: Saws

Q: What boundary-breaking player won the first National League Rookie of the Year Award in 1947?

A: Jackie Robinson

Q: How many films were in the *Rocky* series?

A: Five

Q: What historic club-like weapon often has a spiked metal head?

A: A mace

Q: Which member of *Mötley Crüe* was the drummer: Vince Neil, Tommy Lee, Nikki Sixx, or Mick Mars?

A: Tommy Lee

Q: In golf, what is an eagle?

A: A hole made in two under par

Q: What late-night talk show host's trademark is "Five Questions"?

A: Craig Kilborne

Q: What is the name of Fred Flintstone's boss in the cartoon series?

A: Mr. Slate

Q: In carpentry, 2 x 4 or 2 x 6 pieces of wood spaced at regular intervals within a wall are called what?

A: Studs

Q: What controversial comedian played Ford Fairlane in a 1990 movie?

A: Andrew Dice Clay

 Q: Name the basketball player, notorious for his off-court exploits, who scored the most points in a season with 4,029 in 1961–62.

A: Wilt Chamberlain

- - - - - - - - - - - - - - -

 Q: What band hit the charts with their debut album *Ten* in 1991?

A: Pearl Jam

- - - - - - - - - - - - - - -

 Q: Who played Lando Calrissian in *Star Wars*?

A: Billy Dee Williams

Q: What is an LED?

A: A light-emitting diode

Q: The NBA's Bucks play for what city renowned for its brew?

A: Milwaukee

Q: In what sport might an announcer use a phrase like give and go, garbage time, or picked his pocket?

A: Basketball

Q: Who played the masked character Kato in the *Green Hornet* TV series?

A: Bruce Lee

- - - - - - - - - - - -

Q: The musical group Five for Fighting had a hit song in 2001 named after what superhero?

A: Superman

- - - - - - - - - - - -

Q: Winston Cup and Busch are divisions of what sport?

A: Nascar

Q: In carpentry, the curved claw, the ripping claw, and the shingler are all types of what?

A: Hammers

Q: What is Steven Seagal's occupation in *Under Siege*?

A: Cook

Q: What college bowl game is called the "Granddaddy of Them All," and shares its name with a famous New Year's Day parade?

A: The Rose Bowl

Q: True or false: According to the USTSA, cursing may be called as a violation in foosball.

A: True

Q: What underwear company did graphic designer Nicholas Graham start in 1984?

A: Joe Boxer

Q: What 2001 movie co-starred Jack Black and Gwyneth Paltrow?

A: *Shallow Hal*

 Q: What auto city is the home of Motown Record's original recording studio?

A: Detroit

 Q: In what sport do you use a belay: hang gliding, mountain climbing, or wind surfing?

A: Mountain climbing

 Q: What voice class is singer Luciano Pavarotti?

A: Tenor

Q: In the billiard game of bumper pool, each team starts out with how many balls: 5, 8, or 12?

A: 5

Q: In carpentry, a straight edge is what type of tool?

A: A ruler

Q: What was the full title of the third movie in *The Naked Gun* series?

A: *Naked Gun 33⅓: The Final Insult*